UNWIND

UNLEASHING RAW EMOTIONS

DR. SUMITA MISHRA

MBBS; DNB (PEDIATRICS), PGPN (Boston)
GOLD MEDALIST

INDIA • SINGAPORE • MALAYSIA

Copyright © Dr. Sumita Mishra 2023
All Rights Reserved.

ISBN 979-8-89067-920-8

This book has been published with all efforts taken to make the material error-free after the consent of the author. However, the author and the publisher do not assume and hereby disclaim any liability to any party for any loss, damage, or disruption caused by errors or omissions, whether such errors or omissions result from negligence, accident, or any other cause.

While every effort has been made to avoid any mistake or omission, this publication is being sold on the condition and understanding that neither the author nor the publishers or printers would be liable in any manner to any person by reason of any mistake or omission in this publication or for any action taken or omitted to be taken or advice rendered or accepted on the basis of this work. For any defect in printing or binding the publishers will be liable only to replace the defective copy by another copy of this work then available.

Dedication

This book is dedicated to all those who bottle up the whole world inside them, and a storm takes it all over.

To those witty, chitty, chatty introverts who can speak everything up but not their hearts and minds out. In a world full of biases and judgmental eyes and opinions, this UNWIND is unbiased and nothing but raw emotions of excerpts that life taught us since we were born. Some of these made us lose our mind and soul, some of these devoured our best senses of being, and some taught us the biggest secrets of survival. We all have lots of experiences and exposures every day until we cease to exist, and this book is dedicated to these events of every day.

This book is a dedication to all the students who want to be someone and make their parents proud, those recently adulting who outgrew their childhood and miss it dearly, to express it with memes and statuses, to couples who love each other and those who lost theirs to day-to-day struggles of life, to mothers and fathers working relentlessly to provide for their kids what they never had, to soldiers and their families, to doctors and their families (because this is what my family and I are and what I have experienced like no other), to teachers who taught us survival skills in school (only we realized while adulting), and to grandparents and their boundless love for their kids and grandkids. It's a dedication to nature in its kindest, softest, and fiercest forms, to beauty in delusion and reality. This book is dedicated to human emotions in every situation.

UNWIND is a dedication to life and those living every day and taking notes on making it better by small slices of raw emotions, yet being vulnerable to get their souls bleeding frequently.

Contents

Acknowledgement..9

Preface 11

1. Fury Road...13

2. Yearning 17

3. Escape Hole 21

4. Aftermath of Turmoil 25

5. Wondering Why?! 29

6. Puddles & Emeralds...33

7. Childhood Unplugged 37

8. Sanity..41

9. Fragrances...45

10. Elephant in My Room...49

11. The Rising 53

12. My Ephemeral Being 57

13. Paradoxical Everything...61

14. Altar of Love..65

15. Mysticism 69

16. Audacity 73

17. Cumulus 77

18. Daddy's Li'l Girl 81

19. Introvert Pinnacles 85

20. Aurora in You 89

21. Abendrot 93

22. Storm and Solace 97

23. Seashell's Tale 101

24. The Insignia 105

25. Amaranthine Ardour 109

26. From Fighter to a Memoir 113

27. Iustitia 117

28. Solitude & Shadows 121

29. So Tired! 125

30. Till Eternity 129

31. Cherishing the Roots 133

32. Potpourri 137

Acknowledgement

This book came into existence because of those who gave me existence, Mama and Papa (Subrat Kumar Mishra, IG CRPF, and Meera Mishra), and the sibling without rivalry and my secret keeper (Adisesh Mishra, Lieutenant, Indian Navy). And this is dedicated to the person who encourages and praises me for the tiny things I am good at, my husband (Dr Pinakee S. Kar, Gastroenterologist & Hepatologist), and my darling daughter who made me realize how much love and emotions and empathy I have only after she came into existence (Vedangi).

Immense gratitude to my teachers at school and medical college and my friends (Jaspreet, Dr. Prerna, and Dr. Pallavi for being constants and Dr. Neelam for constantly motivating me), and Disha, my cousin, for being an ardent supporter in all senses and times. Thankful to family, relatives, and in-laws for constantly motivating me.

Thank you so much to the entire team of publication and editorials for this opportunity when I couldn't find a way to make this book exist in real-time without you all.

Always grateful.

Preface

UNWIND came into existence in all its real and solid form when I was pursuing my post-graduation in pediatrics. Only a doctor would truly understand the challenges of the hectic shifts and duty hours during residency in medical education. Well, I've always been a chitty chatty introvert, someone who communicates well externally with people all around but keeps a lot bottled up inside, needing a vent for expression. As a child, I often felt misunderstood, even for the tiniest of things. I'm not blaming my surroundings; it's just that my vocabulary-based expression skills were limited. So, I curated UNWIND as a form of self-healing, like a journal where I could confide without fear of judgment.

My UNWIND won't judge the reader; it's designed to be biased in favour of those who pick it up to read. The warmth of the expressions of emotions will embrace you and provide solace, reminding you that you are not alone in feeling this way about many things.

Enjoy the journey within these pages.

Fury Road

She died ages ago,
What remains is her corpse
Ashes of flesh and bones,
While he roamed with no remorse.

She died ages ago,
Fell for a monster with dual core,
Dreamt of a love nest,
Living in hell made her all sore.

She died ages ago,
Being hit with warm rods, belt and boots,
Bruises all over her back and face,
Screamings even didn't made his heart melt.

She died ages ago,
To chop salad or to slash her wrist?
Warming the milk with eyes on bottle of poison,
To kill self or him or not to kill... Idea dismissed.

She died ages ago,
Family said, "Must be you, we knew!",
On asking for help from family and friends,
Friends convinced her to "Compromise, don't argue".

She died ages ago,
Those dark nights with a drunk demon,
Held her hair, dragging over the floor,
She screamed, untangled and she ran.

She died ages ago,
Clumsily pickup up herself next morning,
To be beaten again and locked up,
Inside her something was slowly burning.

She died ages ago,
When the red eyed lunatic broke her arms,
The screams, pain and agony was so loud,
Yet her neighbors, family and friends remained calm.

She died ages ago,
Wanted to be held by one supportive hand,
Wanted a soul to empathize,
Ironically no one wanted to be around.

She died ages ago,
This time to gather all her courage,
Overpowered his slap, threw his hand away, "Enough" she said,
Left her soul's carcasses and her painful baggage.

She died to be finally reborn,

No more dolled up to hide bruises and scars,

All fiery, enigmatic, ruthless, strong and resilient,

Her timid self was torn, left behind afar.

A Note:

"Many women in India and different parts of the world suffer from abusive marriages, spouses who are drunk or addicted, and the burden of disharmony within the walls of their homes. Often, they become timid and can't stand up for themselves. Neither are they helped by families, friends, nor neighbors. Some are beaten black and blue, and many are even killed during such monstrous violence. Many men suffer the same at the hands of their spouses. Let's eradicate these demons and extend help to such individuals before they succumb to their own remorse."

Yearning

Suddenly places feel vacant without you,
Streets feel lonely & allies empty without you,
Luminosities appear less bright without you,
Faces appear unfamiliar without you,
Jovial moments appear melancholic without you,
Remorse grows over the once made arguments
Smiles brighten thinking of one day less as each pass by.

The places you once lived in with us feels vacant,
The wrinkles so fresh on your left clothes & sheets,
Your fragrances illuminating the pages of your books,
Your used objects, your tea mugs & plates,
The freshly watered plants by you,
The bloomed Li'l buds waiting for you,
The echoes of your voice & laughter,
The portrait with our smiles waiting to be smiles back at.

Your fragrances, voices & memories stay with us,
Your frustrated cries & tears of joy stays with us,
Your thoughts provoke dreams for us to live by them,
Your dreams wait to be cherished by us,
Your tender acts of care remain hung up in the allies of
my soul,

Your soulful voice connects with me asking to hold up a
little bit more,

Your mess ceases to bother me...

Rather makes me smile now,

And we wait for days to come by,

To be as great as ever together,

There is no forever...

This is our forever...

Living today every day is forever...

Still waiting for our forever...

Let's be conjoined souls complementary to each other,

Till forever!

A Note:

"If you love someone worth waiting for, then do wait, because
the notion of 'time and tide waits for none' feels absurd
in such moments. If you love someone unconditionally or
unconventionally, to a degree only you and your soulmates
truly understand, then no explanations are necessary for those
who question it. If you can love someone as if there's no one
else, yet patiently await that one perfect moment, no matter
how long it takes, then it's truly a gift! This love is secure;
it's not bound by time and can transcend time zones and the
problems that may come between you. As they say, only true
love conquers all."

Escape Hole

Let's run away...
From gripping rage,
From solitude & melancholy,
From over dramatic states,
From morbid jealousy,
From erratic mindsets,
From inability to heal thyself,
From inability to repair relationships,
From breakable selfish,
From uncomfortable places,
From elephants in the rooms,
From lacking of help,
From ill sickening judgements,
From drowning sorrows,
From overtly critical views,
And from bad sentiments.

Let's run to seek the good...
For laughters,
For the love of families,
For gratitude,
For calmness,
For soulfulness,

For contributions,

For cooperation,

For being someone's backbone,

For work satisfaction,

For no exploitation,

For helping the needy,

For not being greedy,

For tranquility,

For equality,

For good etiquettes,

For love filled bouquets.

And you'll be remembered....

Long after you're gone,

Being humane & tender,

And not making someone feel alone.

A Note:

"In every scope of self-improvement, we must try. One life to give, love, accomplish, and cherish. So why not! Let people remember you for the kindness and care you provided to those in need... the world needs that more often, because there is a crowd of perfect professionals with perfect qualifications and degrees, with perfect lives, making ample money and living life kindly size, and who just exist for themselves and cease to exist to be forgotten. Be the hero the world and people around really need!"

Aftermath of Turmoil

The grief of ones still trying to stay strong and hold on,

The pain of loss and bereavement forever,

The voids such mishaps create somewhere possibly unimaginable,

The strength to overcome the most disastrous situations,

The permanence of scars which never heal,

The tenderness the deepest of wounds left behind,

The urge to blend in with the crowd just to feel a bit more alive,

The attempts to reach normalcy, to try hard bouncing back, moment there on,

The want to make things easier and better on the other side of the storm,

The memories of loss of loved ones, staring at their belongings,

The wish to go back in time, every time the survivors live the others,

The survivors guilt forever lingering there like creepers all over,

The anticipation of worst happening in near time or future or ever,

The will power to move on somedays and to lie down and
sob the others,

The turmoil making them relive and retell the story of
loss all the time,

The acceptance that it's never easy to stand strong and
cope up,

The learning from the storms and mishaps,

The giving up on "time" and "fate",

It's normal to give in and give up to erase the pain.

It's normal to stay with the scars and tenderness of the
wounds.

It's normal to heal, take your time, sometimes
incompletely.

Broken humans do exist!

A Note:

"Beauty of an approaching storm: Appears deceptively
marvelous to the one that is seeing it from the other side
without the knowledge of how the ocean, the sky, the clouds,
the vortex, the thunderstorms, and other elements are dealing
with the orchestral symphony of minutes before disaster. The
ones who are dealing with the disaster, which looks like a
beautiful piece of art, are the ones who can know the pain, the
loss, and the sufferings of the aftermath.

From the inside of the hurricanes, the picture might be different
for the ones trying to survive it. Onlookers can't possibly
imagine the broken soul and the tethered hearts something

terrible causes to the survivors. While bearable imagination can only depict the momentary sadness, beyond imagination is the being of the broken lone survivors who would still be trying hard to extricate themselves from the harsh memories of the aftermath."

Wondering Why?!

Some minds too twisted to be good to others.

Some eyes too vicious to see purity in others.

Some intentions are too malicious to overcome their egos.

Some souls too corrupt to bridge sour relationships.

Some deeds too heinous to let go of the atrocities creating hardships.

Just wondering then,

What is left in memoirs of that kind of life?

What is left as the purpose to strive?

What is rendered when you depart with the burden?

Can you come back to be a better version?

Can you ease the pain you caused?

Or might press play to buttons you paused!!

So just wondering,

Why can't you undo or unbutton or unburden it?

Why make others' lives horrific and grit?

Why to be perilous and inflict pain on others?

Rather, is it tough to soothe their bothers!?

Wondering mind says,

You don't live for a millennia!

In a blink you just come and go...

Make your presence kind,

Why burden up your corpse with that pent up ego?

A Note:

"Never die with remorse or guilt. Your soul might just never be set free. Never die burdened by the suffering you caused someone in any way. Karma works in mysterious ways, and it's always payback time. The idealistic way of life is the best possible way to set your soul free!"

Puddles & Emeralds

A shallow pond nearby a deep lake,
Inhabited by few seeds of water lilies & hyacinths...
The lake had only pebbles of every hue possible,
Mud of the pond may be the "life factor" I think.

The deep lake had crystalline gallons of water,
Fathomable & palatable mineral water to quench the thirsty...
Where breeze blew and messed with her hair of the wanderer,
While calming the eyes & souls of the observer.

The Pisces, the birds and aquatic plants and whatnots living in,
The sustainable ones inter inter-dependent for residing...
Yet trying to help, sustain & satisfy all,
This lake has an amazing multitude after all.

Meanwhile the jealous pond was feeling timid,
Amidst the vastness of the lake proclaimed by all...
She thought" all I can have is muddy water beneath",
Her mind wanted to grow into the massive lake somehow.

Then one day a frog clan squeezed out,
Few gold fishes swarm across the puddle...
A purple hyacinth bloomed gloriously.
And a few others did appear.

Why did the pond feel timid then?
It wasn't about the vastness or the depth of the lake...
Neither was it about her generosity and allowances...
It was purely about her visible luxury shining far.

Pond rose above it and knew now,
Self worth is variable in varied perspectives...
Envy is never a solution to overcome timidness...
Embracing the good in all & self is a harmonious way to be.

A Note:

"Never envy what you don't understand. Everyone has their own set of struggles and a time frame to overcome those hardships. Just by the mere view of apparent luxury, it can never be judged if the effort behind it was easy or not. More than comparison and self-pity, it is always more important to improvise and channelize our own energies to become a better version of ourselves. Self-pity starts a negative downward spiral of thoughts and actions that pulls us down, makes us underconfident, and questions our abilities. It never helps us grow because there would always be a reason why we can't!"

Childhood Unplugged

Back then, while waking up early...
As alarmed buzzed, running in a hurry...
Wearing the tidy school uniform & hair...
Lunch boxes in bags, with joys to share...
Returning home with mud stains...
School days ended, memories remain...
Innocent faces wearing no cloaks...
Paper boats & paper planes...
Games, fights & ink stains...
Laughing our hearts out at silly jokes...
Back then I wanted schools to be done...
Eager to grow up, thought it would be fun.

Now fake smiles & unwanted laughters exist...
Innocence is no more a gift...
As i grew up, saw many masks over faces...
Purity of character, the chastity was left in traces...
Aging wasn't that adventurous after all...
It's about being in pain yet standing tall...
Being an adult is all a pretentious job...
Carrying burdens while you still can stop...
Forgive and forget they say, yet seldom mean...
A healer, a friend, a forgiver as an adult, is rare to be seen...

Wish I could go back to that era.

Where innocence was intact...

Friends truly kept their words...

What was meant was said in fact...

Where we aspired to reach far beyond the skies...

Where purer were all the ties...

Where school uniforms had wishes & autographs...

And there existed merrier group photographs...

Only if I could keep that child in me intact...

Pure bliss will find its path.

A Note:

"Childhood is all about fun, mess, innocence, ignorance, inquisitiveness, exploitation, questioning, and imagination. In the fast-forward era where everyone is racing at breakneck speed and eager to grow up quickly, will the real essence of being a child vanish? A child is a gift to humankind, an attribute where minds are so much less corrupted that humanity is more intact than what adults seldom have to offer. Let's not grow out of our childhood too quickly. Let's grow up but not extinguish the child within us!"

Sanity

In the darkness of despair,
In the hollowness of being.
In life gone beyond repair,
There was a silent scream.

In the bad state of mind,
In hopeless situations,
In the world so unkind,
It was the beginning of all tribulations.

Lucidity seems gone,
Panic makes him shiver,
Screams in depression,
Noises in head to quiver.

But he was just a youth,
Overachiever but melancholic,
Self hate, agitation, social isolation being his truth,
Neither did he pretend to be jolly.

Insomniac scrolling over gadgets,
Binge eating junk sitting over the couch,
To get over he seldom fidgets,
Crying and yelling at self were heard from his house.

No one bothered to ask him for help,
He was just a gossip for being mad,
Stared the neighborhood for his yelp.
Boycotted him saying his influence is bad.

Once he gives up & decides to end it,
His unmanageable chaotic life,
Failed in situations he couldn't bend,
Job? Love? Situationship? Family? Children & Wife?

No one around knew him enough to gossip,
Yet his life and death both were judged,
What might have helped may be was friendship,
There was no nudge for him, only sludge.

He deserved to live, laugh and be loved,
But adversities pushed him down the roof,
Wishing his first scream, his first social anxiety was addressed, He might have never spiraled in the loop.

A Note:

"In this fast-paced era where everyone wants to run the rat race, it turns out to drain mental health much more than expected. Odd working hours, no social life, doom scrolling, social media, a lack of support in mental health issues, denial, situationships, twisted relationships, etc., and many more in the list add up to it. It's sad that those suffering must be helped and asked to seek help by a psychologist and psychiatrist at the earliest. The more the delay, the bigger the elephant in the room becomes. And what loathes me the most is people who know nothing about the person suffering somehow start judging and labelling him/her. Nudges are like little pushes one needs to grow and overcome procrastination and are much needed. But what people give is sludge, and it pushes the already suffering people over the edge."

Fragrances

Some slender dusky thoughts,
Some nostalgic night scents,
Some chilled night breezes,
Some staring starry creases,
Some chirps of distant crickets,
Some faraway lights flickers,
Some skylines painted meticulously,
Some fireflies hovering ambiguously.
Some leaves & flowers fallen here & there,
Some dreams lived in my head,
Some echoing soothing hums overhead,
Some serenade apparently,
Some myriads of clouds floating by,
Nights like those are never dark,
So many unveilings crisp and sharp,
So much goes unnoticed under the sun,
Hidden treasures mystically reveals before the dawn,
Grieving minds and hearts get soothed,
Unanswered many queries solved,
Feel your alone self breathing and living.
Feel the weightlessness of your being.
Loads get lift from your head,
And burdens from heart,

Can hear your soul answering you back,

Nights and solitudes hug each other,

Seclusion clears up my vision rather,

Drenched in long talks with myself,

Of how things should have been but couldn't be...

And how things are but shouldn't be...

And how things will have to be but can't be!

A Note:

"Many of us like solitude and prefer it. Yet many of us long for someone to be with us on solitary nights with fragrant Jasmine and all types of nocturnal sounds that nature provides. Sometimes, the silence is deafening, and all we wish for is someone to be sitting beside us, comforting. Yet some days when we are surrounded by friends and family, we loathe the gathering and want solitude. Ironically, the soul searches for loneliness, and the body searches for company, with our minds wandering in between like a pendulum clock!"

Elephant in My Room

Expected to sit quite through the anguish,
Soreness to suppress & pile up & banish,
Be despondent about unaddressed issues,
Anger and anxiety, inside they grew,
"Never expect anything from anyone" Echoed,
I felt this notion quite flawed,
"Why not?"buzzed inside my being,
Equal and opposite reaction isn't it THE THING?
Sharing happiness all around,
But in grief & distress no one is found,
When you stood up & by them all,
Why did they let you bruise, bleed, fall?

If Only a soul to emphasize & empower,
If only a shoulder to lean on, ears to hear,.
Healing alone need not be ritualistic,
Helping wounded to stand up, isn't that realistic?
Time heals everything they say,
Shutted down, putting torment away,
Beings never heal, scars are always left,
Time sweeping by through the cleft,
Worst of the pain gets alive,
The moment you take a retrospective dive,

Only the intensity of agony diminishes,
Rarely though the ordeal vanishes,
Both in the fabulous and the flawed,
Pain hurts and healing leaves scars in all,

Only those who challenge their fears,
Only those sewing up all tears,
Only those not blaming the destiny,
Only those ready to fight the mutiny,
Only those empathetic of others suffering.
Only those capable of nurturing.
Only those puzzled enough to question,
Only those giving time to heal,
Only those carrying their scars like medals on chest,
Only those holding on are capable of the best.

A Note:

"Life is all about falling down and getting up again. It's about endeavors and persistence. There are always scars, pain, healing, and strength. It's a process, and people pay prices to learn their lessons through this journey. We need to unlearn a few things to become a better version of ourselves while learning new things. Often, people who are successful don't thank or blame their destiny. They work for it and wear their scars of fall and rise with equal grace. Those who rise almost always gracefully accept their downfalls as flamboyantly as they do accept their rise. Embrace both!"

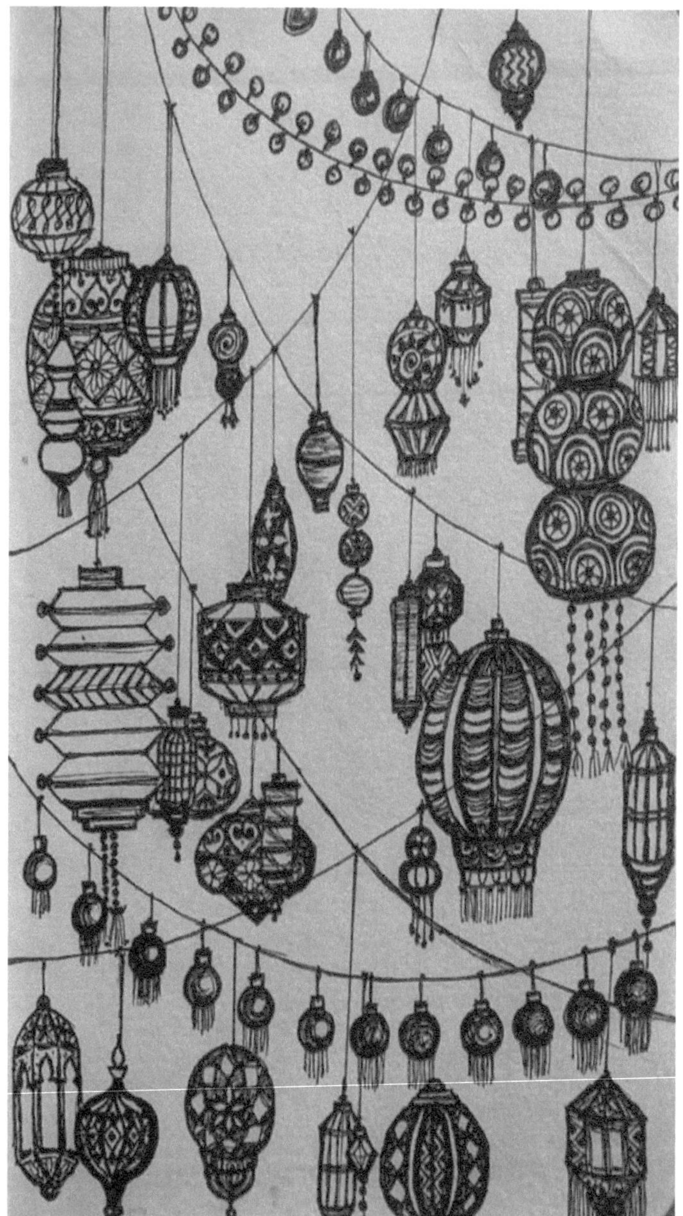

The Rising

Idealism for the youth,
Expected to learn...
Expected to earn...
Expected to serve...
Expected to strive...
Expected to save...
Expected to behave...
Expected to care...
Expected to shine being rare...
Trillions of potentials to unravel may be.

Atmosphere for the same youth,
Exploited at work...
Exploited by all folks...
Exploited by society...
Exploitation for modesty...
Exploited to be idealistic...
Exploited in judgments...
Exploited by comparisons...
Exploitation to toughen...
Zillions of grits & gravels in their path.

Reality of the youth,
Known to be chaotic...
Known to be biased & dramatic...
Known to be selfish...
Known to be immature...
Known neither to care nor nurture...
Known to be a rebel.
Known not to attain their rightful potential.

Are all their behaviors worth it?
Sacrifice of parents...
Sacrifice of finance...
Sacrifice of dreams...
Sacrificing for whims...
Delightfully dysfunctional...
Skeptically delusional...

As 'we' lost our credibility,
As 'we' are categorically chaotic,
As "we" have more failures than triumphs,
Is this how we are built?
Who's then at fault?
Urges to gain insight & introspect...
Give it some time & thought!

A Note:

"While shaping the youth of today from their childhood, parents go through a lot of sacrifices, and I knew this a long time ago, even before I was a parent. But the generational trauma, the scars of invalidation, the denials of fate and fortune, and the adversities of family dynamics made our parents the generation 'who tried to do it for them, their parents, and their kids,' yet behaviorally they have scars that traverse across generations. If being hit for not doing what was told was done to them, they thought it to be the only way. So many millennial parents are here with impacts of generational trauma, trying to unlearn things to befriend their kids and be there so that their kids can trust them. Not blaming anyone or any generation, but that's just the fact. To change the kids and youth, we need to break the cycles of generational trauma and change ourselves first!"

My Ephemeral Being

Everyday She smiled through everything rough...
Inherently her soul was soft yet tough.
While wearing old bruises & scars from past wars
Her smile shined gloriously like ablazing stars.
Never she complained about bad memoirs of the past...
Nor her grin faded in regretting gray clouds that passed.

Until one day she was sun-kissed & touched with love...
She forgot about anything before or beyond her love.
He showed her what was the deficit & where she lacked,
He supported her through...made her again intact.
She smiled...but better than before...with all her soul &
heart...
Not like before where it was hollow...with a background
of impact.

Things went bad when one fine day he left her all alone,
He departed way before...soul remained with her though.
Lost was her beautifully carved self proclaimed eternal
affection...,
Unimaginable deviation...circumstantial deflection.
With feelings of solitude & days spent with despair
Again she slowly got up...healing herself like before.

Only this time she realized she was more wretched & hopeless,

Though she had thousands of battles...some lost...mostly won... never lost focus.

Then why is it this time she was hurt the most?

Was it by losing someone dear you trust??

Looking at her silvery image in the mirror...

She realized nobody lives forever.

Mortality & non dependency answered all her query... Now smiling back she is by setting her soul free.

A Note:

"People come and go. Only you stay with yourself. One day, this mortal realm claims the life of most of us, and we become nonexistent. Loved ones may support you and love you, but you will have to stand on your own and bear the scars of life in the strongest possible way you can, to survive and thrive!"

Paradoxical Everything

Vibrant brilliances...
Yet such silences,
Splash of hues...
Goldens & Blues,
Seeking attention...
Yet liking it lonesome,
Rocky harshness like deserts...
With golden dirts,
Tempting sparkles of lake...
Dreamland seen while awake,
Vastly blue sky...
Watching birds fly,
Lands arid and dry...
Its majestic beauty, hard to justify,
Sustainability is a query...
Living conditions are weary,
Ironically mirages catch attention...
Running behind 'em is a temptation,
Till one reaches near...
Its illusions never clear,
Perhaps its a perceived beauty...
Serving no duty,
Unable to quench the thirst...
Its salty water are a curse,

Rocks unable to grow crops...

Nothing to offer to hungry stops,

Ironies of life...

Hunger & thirst are best perceived...

When you barely survived,

We achieved the harder we strived;

Acknowledgment appears after being deprived Paradox of every existence...

Is just to tell about the other's significance!

A Note:

"If there was no sadness, we would have never known the true value of happiness. If there was no thirst and hunger, the importance of quenching the thirsty or satisfying the hungry would have diminished. To appreciate the power of black, we have to keep our whites the whitest. Everything can coexist and yet embrace and enhance each other's importance!"

Altar of Love

My kind of love might sound obnoxious...
I would love you no matter you want it or not...
Once I promised you my precious...
I will be there for you, be that any spot.

I would love you when we are young and run across treks...
I would love you even if I become old, sick, dead or look terrible...
No matter if they turn their backs on you or you are wreck...
No matter how deeply they hurt you.
Howsoever incurable.

My kind of love will go and protest and detest for your rights...
I would not let you suffer injustices & misjudgments...
I'll hold your hand in crevices, creeks, darkness and heights...
I'll hold your hand when you're irritated & ask me to leave...
I'll hold it when you need but don't ask...
And also, when you need and ask for it.

I would be hurt if people hurt you, your pain becomes mine instantly...

Whether you like it or not, my love gets sad & hurt when people use your goodness and walk away...

I would not like it if people caused tribulations to you constantly...

My kind of love gets sored when your efforts aren't appreciated any day.

No matter they are your family or not...friends or unknown...,

I would still help & support you through them...

My kind of love obeys space, but won't leave you alone in bad days...

I'll still make you smile. Make fun of the world around to make you feel.

My kind of love is not suffocating, it's all about letting go...,

Holding on to great memories.

Support each other through pain...

Letting go the pain by holding on to each other is the agenda...

While Deja Vu of piles of good memories strongly imparts gains.

I would always love you like this whether you want it or not...

I can't "unlove" what is so dear to me you see...

My kind of love is intense like that freshly brewed raw coffee we hadat that hill station...

Nostalgic Aromas growing intensely fragrant that spreads around freely.

A Note:

"While arguing about platonic love vs romantic love, the idealism of platonic love seems so romantic itself. But we are all humans of flesh and blood with hormones and emotions simultaneously functioning, just as the heart and brain coexist. We may not choose either, or we may choose both ways. The best kind of love is the one where you are comfortable with your partner while growing together. The best kind of people don't always get the best kind of love. It's the best kind of efforts that create magical life stories. It's the level of soothing the souls achieve while nurturing each other."

Mysticism

Foggy bewilderments...
Confusing images...
Perplexing echoes...
Delusional enchantments...
Visibility obscures...
Mist never clears...
Appealing aroma...
Confounding loneliness...
Trapping dark muzziness...
Freezing frames...
No sparks...
No flames...
Coldness drilling the bones...
Dark...gray-black-blue monotones...
Out of focusing visions...
Unrecognizable visages
Solivagant wanderers...
Alone in foggy wonders...
Wondering who is more lonely??
Mountains...Mists...or Me??

A Note:

"The quieter you become, the more and better you hear. The more you live consciously with your surroundings, the better it is for your soul and senses to set free and gain the true knowledge of the essence of your being. Being calm and mindful is being truly human. Like in quiet nights, you can hear the crickets chirp, the owls howl, the scent of the moonlight and dew drops on the grass. It's in the quiet, full mind that you can find your true self. Work on yourself to make a better and more beautiful version of you. While the work is in progress, the work that we do on ourselves, we might feel so lonely that it might just drive us mad, and soundless days and nights appear deafening. But self-improvement in every aspect is the essence of our being. That's the purpose of our soul in the mortal realm."

Audacity

How dare is he i must say?
To pick a beter life to stay!

How dare he choose to rise from grit?
To walk away from the normal fit!

How dare is he to rise above all?
When life was painful & dull!

How did he harbour the courage?
Despite the circumstantial gloomy surge!

How dare is he to wake up yet dream?
He was everything but daring!

How did he kept running the race?
Didn't somebody just pull out his shoe lace?!

How did he manage & move further?
Moving forward making his perspective wider!

How dare he didn't stop?
Steadily making efforts till he drops!

How dare is he to don't give damn?
Perhaps by keeping himself calm!

How he not cares about judgements other make?
Don't they give his goals a shake?!

How dare he still finds his path & crawls forth?
He just carried on to make it worth!

How dare is he to make everyone so envious?
Though he never demanded it...
His efforts made it obvious!

A Note:

"People will always remain pissed off at you, not because of you mostly. Many people are pissed off at others because they cannot achieve what the other can. So the natural response becomes denial. They deny your success, they deny your achievements, they deny your identity and existence as someone who made a difference. But even your most vile enemies know what your actual worth and potential are. They are scared to face their own demons. So everyone who has been let down by others, please take a note to self that you scare them and keep going. Do it for yourself, not to prove a point to others. Everyone else will eventually come around, because the greatest battles also cease after years and don't go on forever!"

Cumulus

The ones passing by & floating around...
The ones casting penumbra on the ground...
The ones coming & going in stound...
The ones gray, milky white, some look sunkissed & browned.

Those surpassing things down, flying high...
Those changing hues with the weather & the sky...
Those changing architecture all over, everytime, diversify...
Those detached fluffed, obscuring veils visually pacify.

Be nubivagant, float, change over time...
Climb up the ladders, stand with your heads high, refine...
Choose not to be deluded by the gloomy storms, look out for sunny skyline...
Following your own path, choose your own exemplars...
Make your own paradigm.

A Note:

"You are unique. Create a niche for yourself. There's no need to copy others. No need to chase validation. Instead, try to be like a particular hue from the color palette. So many, yet all outstanding and speaking for themselves alone. There can be only one lavender, only one purple, only one violet, only one lilac, and only one magenta...though they all belong to one family of shades!"

Daddy's Li'l Girl

Opening eyes in her father's arms...

Staring at his great grand smiles,

She was unwelcomed by others...

But her father's eyes had those shiny crystals,

"They" all wanted a son...a heir that day...

Her arrival disappointed "them" all,

Her father would sit hours with her...

Play around, carry her in his lap...

Amidst her restlessness...he took li'l naps,

She was unwelcomed when she spoke for justice...

Girls shouldn't oppose so often "they" said,

Daddy's li'l girl stood alone everywhere...

Like a flamingo in the flock of ducks,

Her righteousness was the gem daddy gave her...

Taught her to cherish it forever,

She was unwelcomed when she worked hard like men...

Also her hopes were crushed now & then,

"They" meanwhile shortlisted criteria for her survival...

Her voice was tried to be shunned & silenced,

She did adjust to what was right only...

In due course she lost friends & family,

Daddy was always there,

Regrets were none...

His virtues were there,

Longing memories imbibed before he was gone!!

A Note:

"This is an ode to all living fathers who love their daughters more than anything and fought with the world to do what's best for his little lady. The fathers who fight against female foeticide, the fathers who graciously welcome their baby girls into their arms, who bring her toys and things to play with, who stay awake with her during sickness and exams, who drive her to the hostel and shed a tear, who give her away in marriage to the love of her life, and similarly welcome their granddaughters as well! It's the heart of a father who can nurture and give away his most prized possession and yet ask for nothing but love and memories! Love you, papa."

Introvert Pinnacles

As I sat & glimpsed at the mighty snow-clad mountains...
The pines, the ferns., the fauna. & also the frozen fountains...

I was mesmerized at the mighty galore & biodiversities...
It all blended in so perfectly despite all imperfections & disparities...

Those pristine sheets of sheer white icy blankets hid so much underneath...
I wondered how nicely it obscured the imperfections beneath...

In the meantime it supported all those dependents requiring shelter from it...
Functioning as one wholesome unit..., though all entities were discrete...

Wasn't the summit just behaving like an introverted child...i was thinking,...
Absorbing the surroundings...it was blending in & sinking...

Yet it had a radiant persona...a personality of its own...
Most of its gallant audacity...from even the farthest it shone...

All I could observe & learn is blend in perfectly... without losing your own peculiarities...

Being generously charming never hurts... always make room for charities...

Keep things under surfaced & upto yourself... when not needed to be unfolded...

And always maintain the dignity people would like to know you for...

That's how the strength of the character is molded!!...

A Note:

"An ode to all introverts. It's often better to remain quiet than to hurt others. It's preferable not to say absurd things and reveal unkindness, rather than saying them to prove that you are mean to people around you. We seldom truly understand what people are going through, so it's generally wiser not to judge and let some people be. Mere acceptance works wonders for all, especially for introverts. They see everything, observe it all, and feel it deeply; they just may not express it verbally and prefer to walk away. An introvert is, in fact, one of the best friends you can have. They will notice your ups and downs, offer their support, watch your back, and include you in their inner circle if you appreciate their quiet and less outgoing nature.

If you connect with introverts, if you are a part of their inner circle, they make sure that you hold a special place in their hearts."

Aurora in You

Neither it's just these spectacular splays of hues emergent...
Nor is it just an interplay of visible particles bringing amazement...

Not that it's just a night sky of both the earthly hemispheres...
It's nature's very own confined yet vast chandeliers...

The dark canopy, sometimes starry...
Sometimes black, gloomy & scary...

Implodes the thought that too much light is blinding??...
Can darkness be soothing? Can too much light be frightening??...

While looking at the candles as I thoughtfully gazed...
Both defying and defining darkness, making me amazed...

It's not just the beauty of the palette making auroras appear so glorious...
How splendidly it transforms the emptiness of the lonely sky into vaults of heaven is marvelous...

Not only it shines apart but beautifies its associates as well...

Enlightenment of oneself while lighting other candles...

Preaching happiness in dark gloomy times...

Keeping hopes high & despair at bay won't cost dimes.

A Note:

"When times are adverse and there is no hope, we tend to view things around us negatively. No matter how much good is happening to us in day-to-day life, in bad days and gloomy situations, they appear insignificant. But the fact is, difficulty changes us all. We grow up a little faster when surrounded by harsh times. The lessons learned in hardships are the ones we mostly never forget, and they not only transform us but also impact the people around us and those related to us. All we need is a glimmer of hope to be our own and others' guiding light and emerge from the dark tunnel, for there is always light at the end of the tunnel!"

Abendrot

Far far away in the mystic land of eternal sunshines...

When the sky lines were painted in purples, saffrons & wines,

Dusk ticked over every minute, nearing the end of another day...

A memoir flashed, when you & me stood watching this splay;

Silence was equivocal, both were equally mesmerized...

You turned back & smiled, my responses were synchronized;

It was a wholeness in your presence that I then attained...

The peaceful soul of yours had my storms contained;

You appeared like a nimbus, an aura, yet amalgamated so well...

I always felt congenial, shared the goods, the bads that I would dwell;

You pulled me out of those quick sands, fixed my broken self...

I too reciprocated back unconditionally for help;

Poles apart in different circumstances, yet attracted like a magnet...

Souls eternally bound, holding each other underneath a protective blanket;

Silences are pertinent, as the briefest encounter unveiled...

Twin flames...!...were we? Resonating together as time revealed;

No one transformed in each other's company, only tried getting better...

No love for their facade, but for the soul's beauty was greater;

Silences are still extraordinary & stillness speaks...

Appreciating sunsets everyday & enjoying those silences... as time ticks...!!!

A Note:

"We all remember our most splendid experiences in our love stories. The smallest of moments that brought us the greatest joy shall always be the ones closest to our hearts. The ones we cherish the most are not grand gestures but simply the small day-to-day acts. Sometimes, a grand proposal or a luxurious gift means nothing compared to a few sips of tea together on a couch, holding hands, watching sunsets, reading beside each other, sharing food on busy days, a small kiss on the forehead, or a gentle hug or pat on the shoulder. These are enough to make you smile on your toughest days. Do cherish such moments, as they are the real gems!"

Storm and Solace

Storms are a chaos borne via cosmos...,

Apoplectic, fiery, enraged, wrathful & furious...,

Disastrous it might seem at the very instance...,

Might awestruck one with its unrestrained brilliance...,

It's a sparkle of unfathomable repression...,

Like humanly nature, which bounces it's boundaries while in depression...,

Small thunders & turbulences gather around when smothered inside...,

Till thresholds are surpassed, then it's nature is no more dignified...,

The brilliance... The wrath...The fury...,

Teaches to take out the emotions, seldom should you bury...,

The aftermath is classier & calmer...,

The peace...The equanimity...The accord... is the real charmer...,

Imbibed in it is the essence of the human soul...,

Yes, a storm teaches life lesson...Once & for all...,

It says hold on till it's too much more...,

Upheaval all...When it's too much...Just pour...,

Afterwards try and stay calm & persist in solace...,

Peace, wrath, rage in life have their own place.

A Note:

"The right expression at the right time is as important as nurturing your baby. Emotions are like infants. We have to let them be sometimes, yet at other times, we have to rein them in. If you parent your baby with mindfulness, they become genuine and resilient, just like your emotions. If you know how to guide and nurture them, keeping them appropriate, life will be calm and filled with equanimity."

Seashell's Tale

Collecting those shells on beaches of those shores,
Lifeless...yet tempting...colorful myriads over the floor,
Brought a few with me for a collection,
Catchy to the eyes...millions, lying like constellations!

Holding 'em in my palm...gleeing like a child,
Staring at the palette & structure, it was then it crossed my mind,
Everyone is so alike yet so different from the other,
Oysters & shells that I collect every summer!

When i grew up,.thought deeper 'bout their significance,
Beyond its external beauty laid its brilliance,
Interpretation was that they served a life so purposeful
Harboring small organisms...symbiosis is so beautiful!

Even after they expired, the exterior beauty tempts the other,
Every single piece of marvel is but different from the other,
Wanna be like those shells, serving helpfully to the needful,
Guess that inner beauty shines outside & fades never!

A Note:

"Some of us are tough on the outside and soft on the inside. It's like a protective mechanism for us. This shields us from getting hurt frequently, as such people often become targets for those who initially seek help and then turn unkind or mean toward the 'shell-like people'."

"It's wiser to help others while setting boundaries, so we don't end up getting hurt in the process."

The Insignia

Left habitual home with all that adrenaline rush at eighteen...
Guts gushing inside made him divergent,
Made him choose the combat uniform, that olive green...
Parents disagreed first, said his thoughts were irrelevant,

Trained, felt, bruised, cried, felt home-sick...dealt all that alone...
All that torment & agony, polishing him to be a combating galant,
Called home to hide the hells of life, the dreaded locus & the unknown...

Stayed away from his own family... smiled at other's happiness... that selfless brilliant,
Stood protecting the nation like a shield, being a backbone...
Insurgency, terrorism, naxalism...all turned his job dangerous & violent,

He never cared, fought for his people, forgot the family survived by him alone...
Years passed...his kids grew up without him...while he was protecting nation...was distant,

Family never complained...briefly enjoyed his presence yearly twice at home...

Grief sticken, tormented...as he heard his mates martyred on way back to regiment,

No family...no friends...yet nation stood above all...rest was all bygone...

Yet he cared about unknown unrelated civilians,

Out of national brotherhood...shaded his own blood...

Since the tender age he vowed protecting those millions,

No matter what circumstances...Wars...earthquakes or floods.

He might not be well perked or well paid...

He might have lost his mates to war, his emotions dead...

He never resented the day he convinced his parents to join forces...

Because his nationalism...his patriotism never

changed its courses!!

A Note:

"To all the bravehearts in the Indian defence forces and paramilitary forces!

It not only takes courage to dedicate a lifetime to serving the nation but also to give every breath and drop of blood for its protection. It's not just the soldiers who are considered tough nuts to crack; the tougher ones are the families always standing behind them like a protective wall. A big salute to those who made the ultimate sacrifice and heartfelt condolences to the families of such heroes. For your loss, we, as Indians, can never repay in any way, but at least we can pledge to be there in all possible ways for those whose fathers, sons, and brothers gave their lives for the greatest cause – nation first, as they say in the forces. (The red poppies symbolize the bloodshed in war, as mentioned in the image above).

Jai Hind!"

Amaranthine Ardour

Everyday I love you a little bit more...
When you smile back at me...
When I'm asleep & you still stare...
In your bright sparkling eyes, my image I see...
When you're home early just to sit by my side...
While sipping tea & silently holding hands...
Your small gestures speak words you can't hide... While
fulfilling my hidden wishes without any demands...
The way you just know what I exactly need...
In between misunderstandings and upsetting days...
Frustrations & tears about what we barely agreed...
Somehow to my heart...you still have your own ways...
Times ahead this love will only grow stronger...
Still sometimes the distance pains & aches...
I feel sometimes we just can't take it any longer...
Hope soon this ice of distance breaks...
Living in faraway lands, longing to meet up...
I can barely not feel your presence nearby...
It's always tougher to keep up...
As I checkered the gone days, feelings intensify...
The way you have your hopes high...
The future that you see for us is brilliant...
Together we grow old, together we die...
Spending a lifetime that magnificent!

A Note:

"They say love is hard to find and harder to keep. It is not just about the honeymoon period; it's about after that period too. It's not just about being in love; it's about staying in love forever. Love is not about beautiful days every time; love is neither about agreements or disagreements, nor is it about standing by each other or walking away to give the other person space. It takes courage to stay in love till the end...till the last breath... knowing the perfect imperfections of someone who belongs to you. It takes belongingness to give up everything every time just to make that one person happy, no matter what it takes out of you. Pure love is that. Pure love is a pure diamond. Shiny sometimes... sometimes not... yet strong and unbreakable! Never let go of such eternal love... even if it takes effort... because it will be worth it!"

From Fighter to a Memoir

Even a fragrant white rose has a black shadow...

A part of her is always hidden away from what they know...

She is both hellfire & holy water...

Only it depends how you treat her...

She wears glory & pain equally well...

She is half goddess & half hell...

The sun watched her through the day...

The moon knew her secrets deep down away...

Her scars were not just a sign of battles she fought They are glorious tattoos of life lessons

being taught...

And it all continued and persisted...

Only to be replaced, thats what time insisted,

Those florets, twigs, meadows, husks n hays, limbs twisted...

Saw seasons, faced wrath of nature, bent down, resisted.,

Some gave up on living, while others still existed...

While the aroma of some blossoms gradually disappears...

New born buds and foliages concurrently appears,

One cycle of life gets over, other one begins...

Blooms & greens changed palettes over the months & years...

Aging brought maturity, meanwhile life escalated upstairs,

Everyone leaves a memoir before going away, then why should the void bother...

Rather have the spirit to remember there sacrifices...be inspired, and live onn,

Time flies by flipping its wings...

Nothing can really replace the importance of the other.

A Note:

"The toughest of the warriors tend to retire one day. Once those who did it all, fought all their battles, and turned the biggest of their foes into admirers, they turn old. Nostalgic tales and lessons learnt remain more interesting, though. People learn from examples of the best and try to stand out. But most of us forget that we all are so very replaceable. For almost everything and everyone, we are just a memoir which they read and re-read and learn a thing or two or unlearn something and move on. Acceptance of this small fact will only release us from the burden of overdoing or over-performing and sacrificing ourselves. The very law of nature is new and better replacing old and good."

Iustitia

The unrisen lunar body, in teary innocent eyes...
One fine night decides not to rise;
Thought God did injustice & bias...
By not giving him it's own light;
Celestial bodies asked "why do you cry?"...
The heartbroken moon said he wanted to die;
Days followed in reclusion & grief...
While stars & planets tried to give him relief;
God soon asked why the moon doesn't arise?...
Others replied he feels repressed & has cried;
The creator went to the moon...
To know the reason he thinks to be doomed;
"Feeling meaningless", replied the orb of the night...
"Why do the sun & stars only have the light?";
The maker smiled & gave him a reflective glass...
If "they" had light... his soothing beauty was beyond passe;
Demiurgic almighty told he gives everyone his own beauty...
Being judicious & just to all is his duty;
How can he refrain his offspring from their dues??
Everyone everytime is born with his own hues;
Luna smiled & accepted himself to be gifted...
Blissfully went back to his duties... with his mood uplifted!

A Note:

"No matter how meaningless and worthless we think of ourselves, our true self-worth is realized when the right time arrives. Even the apparently smallest and least worthy thing might surprise you someday by saving your life, who knows? The universe works in wonderful ways. The point is, we don't understand the big picture and blame our fate for our perceived lack of self-worth."

Solitude & Shadows

How far will you go for something which is not yours...
When unconditional love is all that you provide?
How much more hurt can you tolerate by someone yours...
When they walk away and create a void?

How to live without someone when you never dreamt of separation...
What about the things you have planned to do together?
When for all your care you are misunderstood then...
Is it the time to let go of surrender?

How to force someone who claimed to love you once, to stay...
While killing your self respect, just because you promised...
How to pull together & smile, when your relationship has become stray?
Should you then let go whatever both of you cherished?

You can't unlove somebody who has been your beloved...
Neither can you force anymore to love you like before...
All you can do is keep loving your special one,
No matter how bad it is now...However sore.

If they come through while time passes by.

mostly with intentions to stay...

If they don't catch up & come around, move on...

Just live through the rough day!

A Note:

"Love and possessiveness have a thin line of difference. While love is all about letting the other person be, giving them space, and allowing love to grow and bloom; possession is more about controlling the feeling of love. When we do something for someone with the intent of expecting the same emotions and claim it's love, the truth is it isn't! One-sided love is never a sin, but spending a lifetime not accepting this and making efforts even when roads are closed from the other side is definitely not right. Keep the love that searches for you and treasures you instead!"

So Tired!

Standing tall for so long...
Weeping alone in the crowd...
Telling them all is well while lying...
Helping them while in pain...
Trying to hide the tears...
Limping ahead with a sore soul...
Gripping whatever support hands get...
Laughing just from the outside...
Searching for another soul to help...
While refusing help verbally...
Blinking away the pearls of tears...
Escaping from tremulous precipitants...
Howling from inside to motivate myself...
No one is actually visible for help...
Help is given when seeked by others though...
But Shoulders are not there for those helping hands...
Who will listen?
Who will not laugh?
Who will support?
Whose shoulder is it to rest upon?
Who is there to rely on?
Who will help to seek peace?

Tired soul thinks and thinks...
Tired soul again goes to sleep!

A Note:

"Millennials are very lonely in today's virtual world of social media and tiresome desk job cultures. There is loneliness when they come home from work. On weekdays, the tiresome days drag the physical being, and seldom do we come home cheery and joyful. It's the solitude and the gloominess that makes us so melancholic. Becoming real is really important. Sharing thoughts, life, emotions with real people with whom we can connect is a must to save ourselves in this busy world and virtual life, where we are unsocial in reality and have hundreds of connections on social media!"

Till Eternity

When you would loose your hair & gain nearsightedness...
And I would have lost bits & pieces of my memory,
When you have no work & yet all that bodily tiredness...
And I would have enough time to stare blankly at sceneries,
Would we still remember the good years & laugh?
Or will we cry & be pained that life was tough?

When your joints would creek and spine is bent...
And I would bring us our cups of aromatic brews,
When you would hate to walk yet would have time to travel...
And my hands would be free to paint, craft & sew,
Would we miss the kids around us on being alone?
Or enjoy each other's company when they are gone?

When you would nag and rant over petty things...
And I would be a freak to keep things neat,
When you would cook me meals that were delicious...
And I would read to you daily stoics & affirmations,
Would we relish those moments in the future?
Or hate it that in the past we had no time to nurture?

When you would pluck flowers & pray for hours...

And I wid plant mint saplings in pots & water,

When you take me for long drives of hours...

And I would have an enormous music playlist to offer.

Would we relive our past numerous moments?

Or regret the unfathomable unachieved figments?

Would you like our older selves to love each other more?

Or regret that we couldn't have been there for each other more?

Would you spare me a lifetime to make memories?

Or regret later that we could have made memories?

Would you sit down by my side and smile then?

Or regret that either is sitting alone by then?

Would you live a life & carve a unique slice of life?

Or regret that you lived a busy life like all till you die?

Let's Love. Live. Laugh. Now. Till ever!

A Note:

"The best kind of relationship is when both partners love each other, grow with each other, and spend a lifetime of ups and downs together. Complementing each other while helping each other's growth is as important as mere romance. Holding each other's hand and kisses on the forehead are such beautiful gestures to hold on to. Not all are lucky enough to fall in love and stay in love with that one person throughout their lives. If you are fortunate, cherish it!"

Cherishing the Roots

Scared she was to eat, dance around, work or travel...
Growing in her womb was that pretty li'l marvel.
Her body, her life was never the same as before...
Fitted into maternal dresses, bearing pangs & emotional outpour.

She wasn't a typical maternal or feminine woman ever... Now for her flesh & blood, she was making every endeavor.
Millions of thoughts & dreams being weaved in her mind... Noone teaches you to raise your own baby...
There ain't any pamphlet of institutions of any kind.

Bearing the worst of the pains bathed in that pool of blood... Still smiling while holding her own flower bud.
Waking up innumerable nights to soothe the baby to sleep...
Making her child laugh, taking away the insecurities... while its dark & deep.

Growing up together but not as a symbiotic association...
She gave the child everything with no reciprocal expectation.
When she grew old... needed care & compassion.

All she said was "kid live your life...go...fulfill your passion".

The child went after her words...making her feel proud...

Leaving her alone...waiting...crafting a void.

When he came back...it was too late...

He already lost her to time.

What a bad fate!

Her dementia faded the memories of her most prized possession...

The child still regrets why he made that decision.

That time they spent in childhood were his best memories...

But the mother remembers nothing,

What the child narrates, his mother thinks they are just stories.

Value time before it's long gone...

Sands of time flow away left are none!

A Note:

"Motherhood is beautiful, but the journey is undeniably tough. Every day brings new struggles, whether it's during pregnancy, postpartum, or while navigating life with a toddler, school-going child, preteen, teenager, or as a mother of an adult. What is common for all mothers in all stages is the love and care they shower and the selflessness they exhibit by putting us ahead of everything and keeping themselves at the least priority. Haven't we all experienced childhoods where mothers would make us eat first, even after standing for long hours doing household chores, and then, if food ran out, they'd make do with random snacks or leftovers from the day before? Well, it might not be the most logical thing to do, but it's a demonstration of their care for us and their self-neglect. They often sacrifice their dreams, jobs, aspirations, and 'me time' for the sake of their children and family. It's one of the most unrewarding jobs, considering the tremendous efforts they put into raising good humans and fostering a harmonious family life. So, I believe they deserve love, care, and rest when they need it most, especially as they age.

Salute to the efforts, love, care, and sacrifices of all mothers everywhere. Love you, Mama!"

Potpourri

Our enormous collection of dried foliages,
Left behind with their rustic essence,
Collectibles we are gathering since ages,
Recalling our journey & the bits of reminiscence,

Those springs we traveled to finer lawns,
Lush greens and vibrancy of blooms,
Sitting besides till the dusks and dawn's,
Serenity & peace creeps and looms.

Then came the summers hot horrid humid,
As we walked through those year after year,
Seeking breezy cold brief winds,
We collected some memoirs from there,

Followed the monsoons drizzling by,
Our journey together further creeped
The dampening showers leaving nothing dry
The gushes, the pours, the roars, into the soul all seeped.

As the walks progressed to the autumns,
Yellows, oranges, mustards and browns everywhere,
We gathered merrier times with pine cones, acorns,
Companionship bloomed further in the air.

Into the winters as we entered,

Chilling the spine in those windy snowy weathers,

Journey grew more memorable and affection more tender,

With all those collectible memorials our story is a painter's magnum opus.

A Note:

"Life is a walk to remember, a journey, and not just the destination. So, we rarely remember the starting point and the end point. All we remember is this journey of life with its various seasons of ups and downs, hopes and despair, joys and sorrows. People come along and join us in this walk, and memories become collectibles to cherish. Many of us must have imagined ourselves with our partners in old age, sitting in the garden, enjoying hot beverages amidst the cold breeze, reminiscing about the good old days, looking at old pictures of our family, and laughing merrily. What a wonderful sight, isn't it?"

www.ingramcontent.com/pod-product-compliance
Lightning Source LLC
Chambersburg PA
CBHW031417150726
47989CB00002B/689